"You don't whisper anymore."

"I'd invite you in, but my life's a mess."

"Either cheer up or take off the hat."

"There's someone I'd like you to meet."

"Good morning, beheaded—uh, I mean beloved."

"Why am I talking this loud? Because I'm wrong."

"The sixties are over, Ralph. The seventies and the eighties, for God's sake, are over. Give it a rest!"

"It's a check for a hundred thousand dollars. Do you like it?"

"Leon, do you think it's all psychological?"

"Because my genetic programming *prevents* me from stopping to ask directions—*that's* why!"

"You smell like a chimney."

"There has been a sharp increase in his cantankerousness."

"We're fighting like—well, we're fighting."

"We're pushing forty. Shouldn't we have a house, or something?"

"Often, it's sullen and withdrawn, and then, suddenly, it becomes hostile and vengeful."

"What happens when *I* become a reality?"

"So now all of a sudden you're *Mr. Spontaneous.*"

"As a matter of fact, you did catch us at a bad time."

"He's like, 'To be or not to be,' and I'm like, 'Get a life.'"

"This time, I'm skipping love and looking for value."

"Merry Christmas."

"Same to you."

"It's all about power—getting it and keeping it."

"Tightening the buttocks."

"Let's stop this before we both say a lot of things we mean."

"I think older women with younger men threatens all the right people."

"It's not you, Frank, it's me—I don't like you."

"I have two children from a previous sexuality."

"We, the jury, find the defendant guilty of killing her softly with his song."

"Don't you understand? I love you! I need you! I want to spend the rest of my vacation with you!"

"Sorry, David, but I'm strictly catch-and-release."

"We laugh at the same things."

"Not tonight, Howard, but you <u>have</u> advanced to the next round."

"Damn! He took the car keys with him."

"He's interesting. But he's not Brazilian-bikini-wax interesting."

"This place is one of New York's best-kept secrets."

"Would you like to come up for a margarita?"

"And do you, Barry, take this woman, warts and all, to be your wife?"

WILL ROBOTS EVER REPLACE MAN?

| WORKBOT | COMMUNICATORBOT | SEXBOT |

"Trophy husbands."

"We had an argument, and now he's trying to make me feel bad."

"My concession speech will be brief. You win."

"Of course, all the good ones are fixed."

"*Our marriage is undergoing something of a renaissance.*"

"I told him it wouldn't kill him to try to be nice once in a while, but I was wrong."

"When did our relationship move from the bedroom to the kitchen?"

"Just six months ago, he was completely feral."

"Of course I'm listening. I'm in a heightened state of alert."

"Now, isn't this more fun than spending money on dinner and a movie?"

"O.K., *step away from the laptop and hold up your end of the conversation.*"

"Can't you ever relax?"

"To really get to know someone, you've got to divorce them."

"I don't care if she is a tape dispenser. I love her."

"And in this corner, wearing the blue trunks, weighing in at a hundred and seventy pounds and insisting that the dining room should not be decorated in lime and oak tones but, rather, with a pastel canary-yellow and walnut trim . . ."

"Wow... We could really fill this room with uncomfortable silence."

"I had a nice time, Steve. Would you like to come in, settle down, and raise a family?"